Spark: Igniting a Culture of Multiplication

by Todd Wilson

Edited by Lindy Lowry
Foreword by Dave Ferguson
Collaboration by Daniel So
Cover Design and Layout by Karen Pheasant and Story.GS

Special Thanks

I want to thank each of our sponsors including Exponential, Zondervan, and Intentional Impact for their role in making this resource available for free in digital form. They are fantastic partners in ministry. Please check out their websites and consider sending them an email of thanks!

Lindy Lowry, Daniel So, Karen Pheasant and Eric Reiss you were instrumental in helping create this new resource. You are the best at what you do.

Larry Walkemeyer: Your personal journey toward multiplication, your passion, your encouragement and your kindred spirit on this important topic provided the inspiration needed to keep this project moving to completion. Thank you Larry.

Bob Buford: Thank you for doing for me what Peter Drucker did for you. I'm grateful for having a front row seat watching you live out a personal culture so powerfully aligned to your core values and convictions. You are a great role model for the alignment model discussed in this book.

Alan Hirsch: Encouraging me to write when it's just about the last thing I'd chose to do.

Bobby Harrington: Being a great friend who was willing to challenge me to a rewrite that made all the difference.

The team at Exponential: Terri Saliba, Bill Couchenour, Jan Greggo, Karen Gilley, Lauren Lee, Brooks Hamon, Stephen Erwin, Dave Ferguson, Don Smith and Pat Masek. Wow! You are the greatest team in America. Your dedication, sacrifice and servant hearts to help church planters make you the heroes to the heroes you serve!

Finally, my wife and partner Anna, for your encouragement during this heavy season of writing.

EXPONENTIAL
CONFERENCE
2015
April 27-30 | Tampa, FL
October 5-8 | Los Angeles. CA

🔥 At **Exponential 2015** we will pursue together how to use our **Tensions** to shape a **Culture** of **Multiplication**

- 100+ Speakers
- 9 Tracks
- 5000 Church Planting Leaders
- 10+ Pre-Conference Forums & Labs
- 20+ Bonus Sessions

REGISTER AT:
exponential.org/2015

Spark: Igniting a Culture of Multiplication

Table of Contents

Foreword

Multiplication and movement making have been the constant conversation upon which my great friendship with Todd Wilson has been built. When I first met Todd, he was the Executive Pastor of New Life Christian Church and he wanted my help to multiply this new church into several locations across the Washington D.C. area. A few years later, we skipped the main session at a conference, sat down together and scratched out a model for how to multiply churches through networks.

It was a good day eight years ago when Todd asked me to partner with him to lead Exponential where our mission is to accelerate movements. It has been a privilege to work alongside Todd and I can't think of anyone more qualified to write this book, *Spark: Igniting a Culture of Multiplication*, than him.

When people ask me about Todd, my first response is, "Genius!" For those of you who know Todd, you are nodding your head in agreement. For those of you who don't know Todd yet, you are about to find out what I mean. As you read *Spark*, you will discover the remarkable insight God has given him. When you get to chapter four about the tensions of moving to multiplication thinking, you will find out exactly what I mean; where most of us would struggle to articulate two or three tensions, Todd gives us 17! His mind thinks like that - all the time. It is a God-given gift and we are fortunate to have access to it.

A second word that comes to mind in describing Todd is Futurist. Every bit of this book is leaning into future and describes who the church needs to be and what the church needs to do. Todd has a unique ability to see over the horizon and know what is coming next. He will often start a phone conversation with me by saying, "I have a hunch…" or, "My intuition tells me…" and I know that God has given him a glimpse of the future. In *Spark,* you get a peek into God's preferred future for the church. God wants his church to be one that multiplies, moves the mission forward and accomplishes the Jesus mission. Read *Spark* and follow it into a better future!

Maybe the best word that describes my buddy, Todd, is Apostolic. He is someone who loves Jesus, loves the church and works tirelessly to see the mission advanced. This book was written with that sole motivation from the heart of an apostle. Todd could have dedicated his talents to other endeavors and made piles of money, or gained tons of influence for himself. Because Todd loves Jesus, the church and the mission, he has dedicated his gifts to the cause of Christ. If the apostle Paul was alive today and writing a practical guide for today's church, I believe he would write something very similar to *Spark: Igniting a Culture of Multiplication.*

Thank you, Todd, for yet another conversation on the topic of multiplication and movement making. And thank you for typing this one out so we can share it with the rest of the world.

Dave Ferguson

Introduction

The Church of Jesus: the most imperfect perfect plan in eternity. Perfect because of the One who dreamed it, founded it, leads it and equips it. Imperfect because of the sinners He calls to steward it, to manage it and to call it home.

This book is for the heroes of the faith who follow their calling to lead in the local church, God's chosen instrument for carrying the fullness of Jesus into every crack and cranny of society. The subsequent books in this FREE eBooks series are a celebration of multiplication written by practitioners who are bucking the status quo and igniting cultures of multiplication. Many are leaders you've probably never heard of, flying under the radar. Make no mistake, these leaders are doing remarkable things amid all of the same tensions you and I face in church leadership.

You know the joys and the struggles of leading a community of faith. It's often a thankless role that leaves you with more questions than answers, and more doubts than affirmations. You have God and the power of the Holy Spirit on your side, but if you're honest you still struggle with a mile-long list of challenges and difficult people—challenges that easily discourage you. And if you're not careful, these challenges tempt you to focus your attention on the wrong things and develop unhealthy paradigms. Even worse, you might be idolizing other leaders, their models and their strategies.

At first glance of the topic and message of this eBook, you might mistakenly shy away from reading it. Who wants to spend their time and energy to learn about one more thing they're not doing well? I get that. But let me encourage you to press through that fear. This eBook is more about putting to death unhealthy thinking and paradigms, and less about creating great strategies.

Pause for a moment. Take a minute to write down the three most difficult tensions you face in your unique context. Don't write down the challenges of the day. Go deeper to the two or three tensions that live with you—the ones you lose sleep over and find

11

yourself stressing about the most. Give it some thought. Maybe they're tangible tensions like having enough money to survive or enough leaders to grow, or discerning how you'll do the next outreach campaign. Maybe it's the effectiveness of discipleship and your struggles to call people to a radical, life-changing encounter and journey with Jesus. They could be today's realities or possibly potential obstacles in the future. You have tensions. Everyone does, including the most successful church leaders you follow.

If you take nothing else from this eBook, embrace the truth that your tensions are normal. They will follow you all the days of your life, including your ministry. Jesus promised, "in this life, you will have trouble" (John 16:33). Tensions are part of the plan God uses to grow you. What matters is how you see beyond and grow through these tensions and challenges.

You are creating and cultivating a culture in your church. There is no stopping it. Just as the sun rises and sets each day, your core values and convictions are always there transforming your thinking into actions that functionally form your church's unique culture. How you face and maneuver through the tensions you experience might be the most significant blessings you have in shaping your church's culture and DNA.

Like the small rudder on a large ship directing the ship's course, the stewardship of the culture/DNA in your church may be the most profound role you play as its leader. Tensions are inseparable from the culture you cultivate. Embrace them as a blessing.

Pause again and reflect. What culture are you creating? Not the seemingly elusive culture you want to develop, but rather the real culture you're creating by your thinking, actions, and the models you pursue. Are you developing a subtraction, survival, and scarcity culture characterized by, "We will [fill in blank] *after* we grow or can afford it?" Or maybe an addition growth culture characterized by an insatiable drive for conquering the next hill and breaking the next growth barrier. A culture characterized by,

Spark: Igniting a Culture of Multiplication

"Where is the next one?" Or are you bucking the norm and creating a multiplication growth culture? A culture best characterized by release versus consumption, and movement versus accumulation?

Your specific culture (subtraction, addition or multiplication) is formed not by who you want to be in the future, but rather by who you are and what you're doing today. The collection of small, consistent daily decisions are each a stone in the foundation of the culture you foster. Want a multiplication culture? Figure out how to multiply in your setting today. Research shows us that when a church waits for an elusive day in the future to start leaning into multiplication, that elusive day never comes.

"But that just doesn't seem practical in my setting. I'm struggling to feed my family and don't have the resources to think multiplication." Let me remind you that leadership is about seeing a preferable future and putting practices in place today that move things toward that future. Our sense of scarcity is in part shaped by our paradigm of addition growth. We watch closely what growing churches are doing and many times incorrectly assume those practices are what we should be doing. When the resources required for addition growth simply aren't there, we become discouraged. This path paralyzes church leaders, further exacerbating a survival culture.

Let's get real, though, and put some skin on these ideas. Consider Dan Smith, founding pastor of Momentum Christian Church in Cleveland, Ohio. Like most planters, Dan started Momentum in a scarcity setting. He assessed his personal strengths and questioned whether he would ever be a megachurch pastor. Dan had a choice to make. Would he wait for the elusive day when Momentum could afford to participate in multiplication? In the spirit of the words of Joshua in chapter 24, Dan concluded, "As for me and my church, we will multiply! Not in a few years, not when we can afford it but from this day forward."

Instead of measuring accumulation (attendees, worship services, giving, etc.), Dan began to measure "sending" impact. He chose to highlight and celebrate the number of leaders Momentum sends to plant churches and be part of church planting teams. Any regular attendee at the church knows the scorecard and the current stats. In just a few short years, Momentum has sent more than 100 people to plant churches and be part of church planting teams, while running several hundred in regular attendance. The day will come when they've sent more people than they have in attendance. That is multiplication—with no prerequisite to "grow and be established" before they started to think multiplication!

Here's the reality of Dan's decision. Already, his impact is greater than most of the churches on the various church growth lists out there. And the culture they've created has exponential potential to harvest. Truth is Momentum Christian Church's story can be your church's story with no waiting to grow and "be established."

Don't miss this: The powerful mechanism behind Dan's approach is not his specific model or method. Instead, it's a wholehearted commitment to a set of values and convictions that shapes all he does. It's a powerful filter for shaping what they celebrate and the practices they put in place. It's an aligned culture rooted in multiplication.

Think about the strong alignment between your core values, the stories you tell and celebrate, and your practices. At Momentum, the culture is so bent on multiplication that church attendees don't have to be there long before they're asking themselves, *What number will I be? Will I be the 130th disciple to go and help multiply?* The culture there fuels itself like a rolling snowball, picking up increasing speed and energy. The DNA is embedded in each person sent—creating a chain reaction that can't help but multiply into the future.

Dan could have embraced addition growth as his target, and waited for all the stars to align before multiplying. Instead, he looked beyond the scarcity setting and began acting today, consistent with the culture he wanted to create in the future. It's the only way to break out of an unhealthy and/or limiting culture—a culture that potentially constrains what the church is designed to do.

My objectives in writing this book are narrowly focused: to highlight the prominent church cultures you most naturally create; to challenge you to candidly assess which culture you are cultivating; to encourage you to put to death some of the paradigms that drive our idolatry for faulty cultures; and to equip you to surrender your current paradigm for the abundance and fruitfulness of a multiplication culture.

Your tensions are real. So is your culture. You can't always change your context or the hand you've been dealt, but you can change your thinking. And that is the catalyst for changing your culture.

Lets get started!

Spark: Igniting a Culture of Multiplication

Chapter 1 - Add *and* Multiply

"Be fruitful and increase in number;
multiply on the earth and increase upon it." ~ God

My friend Rick Ruble loves to play the board game Risk. I actually dislike the game, but because of Rick's competitive nature and passion for it, I've played a few times. I don't remember how to play or even much about the game, but I do remember Rick's passion in saying, "Think globally, act locally" repeatedly. The strategy fueled his nearly perfect winning record.

Another way of paraphrasing this strategy is, "you must have a micro or local strategy close to home for *adding* the next one, and simultaneously a macro strategy for *multiplying* your impact beyond your local context." The two must work in synergy.

The principles of this simple strategy actually come from Jesus and His Commission to make disciples (Matt. 28: 19). We must have a local or "micro" strategy that is reproducible and works at the individual disciple level. The truth is that all multiplication has addition at its core: reaching the "next one." Jesus handed down a model of personal discipleship and evangelism that is solidly addition growth. Our local or micro strategy in church must be to create environments where each and every follower of Jesus can participate in addition with a focus on their personal sphere of influence.

At the same time, we must simultaneously and intentionally have a "macro" strategy that looks beyond our local context and seeks to extend and multiply churches. The macro strategy recognizes that the most powerful way to multiply is to create new churches that become platforms for addition at the individual Believer level. Macro results give new contexts and frontiers for micro strategies, and it's the micro that wins new people to Jesus. The micro (addition) and macro (multiplication) must work in tandem.

Healthy Growth

We must add. We must grow. We must reproduce. In doing all three, we create a powerful process in which *everyone* is focused on "the next one"—the next disciple, the next small group, the next church plant. Because we win people to Jesus one by one, as church leaders we need to create environments that foster *everyone* adding disciples. Growth is a good thing.

But at the same time, we need to look toward the horizon and grasp the reality that radical multiplication only happens when we release and send people rather than only catching and accumulating. Our "macro" approach must look for simple strategies to replicate the Church into new places and new contexts where the "act local" addition can then do its thing.

So how do we pursue the addition (micro) and multiplication (macro) simultaneously? It starts with intentionality. We must purpose to continually ask ourselves, "How do we help everyone in our church reach their 'next one'?" while simultaneously asking, "How do we release and send people to reach the next 100,000?"

Movements represent the intersection of a healthy balance between the addition and multiplication strategies; a movement multiplies through addition, with life-on-life and one-on-one relationships offering the best context for adding disciples. The micro (or local) does the heavy lifting of adding while the macro (releasing and sending) gives the context for multiplying. It takes a unique culture to fuel multiplication and movements thinking.

The Way of Jesus

At this point, you may be skeptical. You may be thinking, *show me the biblical basis for this addition (micro)* "and" *multiplication (macro) thinking.* Let's take a closer look into Scripture.

After the flood, God told Noah, "Be fruitful and increase in number; multiply on the earth and increase upon it." It's reasonable for us to conclude that the increase comes through some combination of addition and multiplication. There are no other pathways to "increase." At a minimum in the context of God's command, the increase refers to our understanding of addition.

It's also reasonable for us to conclude that the family unit was God's design and plan for repopulating the earth. The family unit provides the mechanism for "increase" through reproduction and the union of a husband and wife.

Pause and look at what God did *not* command and what did *not* happen as the earth was repopulated. God did not say to Noah, "I will give you 6,000 years of life to grow one huge family with billions of children." Instead, God established a micro strategy via the family where children would be "added" to individual families. Those children would develop, mature, and eventually be released and sent to establish families of their own (macro level). From 1 to 3 to 9 to 27 to 80 and beyond. Multiplication spreads far and wide while addition accumulates tall and narrow.

The micro or local strategy for increase is addition through the family unit. The macro strategy for increase is multiplication of families to the ends of the earth. Each multiplication of a family at the macro level provides a new context for addition at the micro level. Sound familiar?

Let's look at a second example. Jesus spent three years discipling twelve men. He modeled his "micro" or local strategy for increase. He showed them a powerful addition strategy for adding the "next one." Life-on-life discipleship living in community together. He then activated His Church as the basic context for addition; a family unit. Just as the family unit provides a powerful mechanism for adding new children, the Church functions in a similar way, sending disciples to multiply new churches.

Spark: Igniting a Culture of Multiplication

Jesus commanded His disciples to, "Go and make disciples of all nations":

> *"You will be my witnesses in Jerusalem, and in all Judea and Samaria,*
> *and to the ends of the earth."*

Look at what Jesus did *not* say and what the disciples did *not* do as His witnesses to the ends of the earth. Jesus did not say, "Stay in Jerusalem and build an ever-bigger church." Nor did He say, "focus most of your energy on accumulating." Instead, He commissioned us to "make disciples," His micro or local strategy to happen wherever the church is. But He also said, "Go to the ends of the earth as you do it." That is a macro multiplication strategy. To stay in Jerusalem and build a bigger and bigger church would be a macro addition strategy.

In this context, the micro strategy for increase is addition through discipleship at the local level within the church. The macro strategy for increase is multiplication of disciples to the ends of the earth. Just like each multiplication of a family at the macro level provides a new context for addition at the micro level (the family strategy given to Noah), each multiplication of a church at the macro level provides a new context for addition of disciples at the micro level. There is a powerful synergy between the micro and macro strategies.

As I mentioned earlier, Jesus Himself gave us the addition (micro) and multiplication (macro) design for His Church. How we respond and embrace this design becomes a significant factor in shaping the growth culture we develop in our churches.

The Opportunity

We have two cultures that can emerge as we pursue growth:

Addition Growth Culture = Addition (micro level) + Addition (macro level)

or, as illustrated in the examples of Noah and Jesus:

Multiplication Growth Culture = Addition (micro level) + Multiplication (macro level)

In both cases, we are commanded to make disciples at the local or micro level. We are to create churches that make disciples and teach people to trust, follow and obey Jesus. Notice in the two equations above that it's the macro level focus making the difference between the two cultures. We get ourselves in trouble when the micro and the macro strategies are simultaneously rooted in an addition.

What does it look like to have micro and macro strategies both focused on addition?

In the case of Noah's mission to repopulate the earth, the micro strategy would produce the normal offspring within Noah's immediate family. In a macro strategy of addition, Noah would become a patriarch focused on building a larger and larger family by accumulating more and more children within his family. Instead of being sent to start their own families, his children would be put to work supporting and helping to grow the infrastructure required for a larger and larger family. Sending children to start their own families would be the exception to the rule and happen infrequently. Sound absurd and unnatural? It is. But this is exactly what we do in the church when we create an addition (micro) / addition (macro) culture.

So what would it look like if Jesus' way for the Church was

21

addition (micro)/ addition (macro)? In that scenario, the local church would grow through the addition of disciples via the micro strategy of discipleship. As these disciples learned to trust and obey Jesus and become more like Him, the church would accumulate and use these mature disciples to resource additional addition-based strategies rather than releasing and sending them. Instead of creating new capacity for additional micro addition via new churches, the resources would be used in building ever-larger existing churches. It would be like Noah rarely sending his children to start families of their own, opting instead to repopulate primarily through his own efforts.

See the problem? When our macro strategies focus on accumulating and adding rather than releasing and sending, we get addition growth culture rather than multiplication growth culture.

We have three key challenges (or opportunities) before us:

- First, a growing number of leaders are questioning the quality of our disciple-making efforts at the local or micro level. Are we producing fully devoted and surrendered disciples who would go and start new churches if called and sent? While this is a significant issue, we're not addressing it in this eBook. (You may want to check out Exponential's 25 free eBooks on discipleship.)

- Second, macro multiplication strategies are by far the minority to addition strategies. Most churches default to macro addition-growth cultures, opting for accumulating more staff, larger facilities, more sites, etc., rather than creating a culture of releasing and sending. Today's average church tends to champion catch and accumulate over release and send.

- Third, as a result of the first two items above, our prevailing church cultures are addition-growth cultures rather than multiplication-growth cultures.

As we look at multiplication and champion the increase in radically multiplying churches, I want to be clear here that this conversation is not anti-growth. Both cultures above—addition-growth culture and multiplication-growth culture—involve growth. I've tried to be careful in this eBook to compare and contrast "addition-growth culture" with "multiplication-growth culture" rather than pitting growth against multiplication.

Exponential's dream is to see an ever-increasing number of churches embrace multiplication growth cultures. This must start with church leaders looking hard at the macro level strategies they embrace. Are you embracing a macro-addition strategy or a macro-multiplication strategy?

In the next chapter, we'll take a deeper look at the differences.

Chapter 2 - Unpacking Our Prevailing Cultures

Something's Just Not Right

My personal angst did not happen over night. It has been growing for several years and is still coming into focus. I'm a product of the church growth movement and support the best of our addition-growth culture. I've been part of it and will continue to champion it. However, I've come to believe that this addition-growth culture is incomplete, and potentially a barrier to real multiplication growth.

It's easy to find wildly successful growing churches doing all the right things for addition at the "micro" or local church level. It's far more difficult to find radically multiplying churches like Ralph Moore's Hope Chapel who are experiencing and igniting multiplication growth. Today, more than 700 churches can trace their roots to the seven churches Ralph started. That's multiplication! Far more significant than the current numbers is the reality that those 700 churches have multiplication so deeply embedded in their DNA that the resulting additional churches—which will be started over the next 10 years—will likely be mind-blowing.

For now, lets define "radically multiplying" in a way that is so different and so aggressive—compared with our current paradigms and measures of success—that few people would argue whether it's addition or multiplication. The fruit of these churches is such a testimony that these congregations are radically multiplying without the need for a definition.

As we press into our Exponential 2015 theme of igniting a culture of multiplication, our team set out to identify ten radically multiplying U.S. churches. Just ten that we could highlight and learn from. With more than 350,000 churches in the United States, that ten represents just .003 percent of churches. We spent months looking and inquiring, but we couldn't find ten. We couldn't find even three.

Something is just not right. If the church is made to multiply, why don't we see it?

With most every problem comes the promise of opportunity and change. Church leader/planter, you are perfectly positioned, amid all your struggles and tensions, to be a change maker. That may sound counter-intuitive, but it's true. That change starts with embracing new ways of thinking. Moving the needle from less than 0.005 percent to greater than 1 percent and then to 10 percent will take a groundswell of next-generation leaders like you who will look beyond the prevailing measures of addition growth and adopt new scorecards of multiplication growth.

Perfectly Aligned for our Results

Organizational culture is a powerful thing. Eventually, our practices adjust to align with what we value the most and the stories we celebrate.

It's far easier to find innovative, growing churches doing externally focused activities, multisites and some church planting with a macro addition-based culture than it is to find churches with a macro-multiplication culture. Consider the growing number of Top 100 church growth lists that celebrate addition growth. As we combed through the most recent lists of the largest and fastest-growing churches, we were struck by the absence of radically multiplying churches.

Do the exercise yourself. Make a list of the top 10 most influential churches you can think of in the United States. These churches are likely doing remarkable things and positively influencing the Kingdom. But how many are radically multiplying? How many are sending more staff than they are keeping? Putting more money into church planting than facilities? More aggressively planting churches than launching multisites? How many can trace 500+

existing churches directly to their roots?

You get the point. We've defined success as addition growth, and few would argue that we've adopted it as our prevailing value that transcends most all we do. As a result, our practices and the things we celebrate align to produce what we value: an addition-growth culture.

In their book, *Viral Churches: Helping Church Planters Become Movement Makers* (based on findings from Leadership Network's State of Church Planting study), authors Warren Bird and Ed Stetzer spell it out for us: "In spite of increased interest in church planting ventures, there has yet to be a documented church planting movement, which involves the rapid multiplication of churches rather than the simple addition of churches."

Stetzer and Bird go so far as to call this pursuit of growth an "addiction."

"Our 'viral church' idea is about falling in love with multiplication and abandoning what seems to be an addiction to addition," they write.

Our addiction to addition growth starts the minute a new church is launched. LifeWay President Ed Stetzer has done extensive studies on church planting (health and survivability). His 2007 study on church survivability reported the following:

- The average new church launches with approximately 40 people and grows to 80 in five years. It receives approximately $40,000 in outside funding to get started and approximately $80,000 in the first four to five years.

- The average church then plateaus at the national average attendance of approximately 90 people by the seventh or eighth year.

- Approximately 68 percent of churches are still alive after four years. However, nearly 40 percent of those surviving until year four are not financially self-sufficient.

By adding in a few additional realities and assumptions, we can reasonably conclude the following:

- The first seven to eight years of the average church plant lives in a scarcity and survival culture. That is reality.

- Addition growth becomes a perceived necessary strategy and focus for survival. The church planter is keenly aware from day one that the new church will not survive if he/she does not grow from their small start of 40 to at least 80+. Before their survivability is even known, the rut of addition growth is firmly established in new churches.

Behavioral specialists would likely draw a strong link between this addition startup culture and the average U.S. church plateauing at fewer than 100. Here's the logic: It takes 90 to 100 members to financially support a staff position. Likewise, one staff person has the capacity to support the activities, programming and shepherding of about 100 people. A church growing to 80+ people in the traditional paradigm will hit a lid of growth due to staffing capacity when it reaches 80 to 100 people—exactly in the range of the national average church size. The plant concludes they need to "add" staff to "grow." Unfortunately, their paradigm becomes, "We can't add staff *until* we grow. We can't afford it." In being constrained by the paradigms/models of today ("paid staff do the heavy lifting" and "we can only do what we can financially afford"), the church paralyzes itself at fewer than 100 people.

These dynamics start the cycle of "feeding the beast," a characteristic underpinning of an addition-growth culture, and foster the great professional/laity divide. The progression goes something like this:

Launch into Subtraction/Survival Culture >> Graduate to Addition/Accumulation >> Become Stuck in More Addition

If this progression naturally led to and culminated in multiplication growth, we might have cause to celebrate. Unfortunately, more addition growth does not naturally lead to multiplication. In fact, the activities that produce more addition growth can actually inhibit or become a barrier to multiplication. This might help explain why upwards of 20 percent of U.S. churches are in an addition-growth culture, but less than .005 percent has graduated to a radical multiplication culture. To add further challenge, our next generation of leaders looks to the 20 percent as their role models for what it looks like to have a successful church.

We've all heard the adage "the definition of insanity is to keep doing what you've always done and expect a different result." It's time to change the way we think.

Reviewing Some Basic Mathematics

When it comes to church growth and church planting, we routinely use common terms: "subtraction," "addition," "multiplication," "growth," and "reproduction." We tend to adopt our own definitions based on our unique context for church. Our temptation might be to look at our success with addition and making Top 100 lists and incorrectly conclude that we are multiplying. Or to look at our church size and mistakenly conclude we can't be a multiplying church if we're small.

Let's start with a very simple and basic review of some mathematic concepts. Rather than making up our own definitions, I'm embracing the terms that have been handed down to us through mathematics. (Don't worry if you did poorly in math; just grab the core concepts.) I realize some of you may be saying, "Before I get into this section, give me the biblical basis of this math!" I would just remind you that the same God who communicates His words through the Bible also created nature and mathematics. These are not "secular or business" concepts but rather the principles that emerge from God's creation.

29

As you look at the following series of graphs, focus on how the output result or number (#) changes with time (the input effort). The input effort represents some combination of your time, your talent (or applied effort) and your treasure (your financial resources). Subtraction, addition, multiplication and exponentials are all distinguished from one another based on what happens to the output result or number (#). How does the output result change as input increases (that is, what happens to the output result as you move to the right on the graph)?

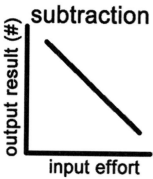

Subtraction. In the Subtraction culture, the output result (#) decreases with time (or as the input effort increases to the right). As the graph shows, every positive unit of input effort results in a loss or "subtraction" in the output number (#).

We all know the pain of seasons of subtraction and loss. On the personal front, to lose loved ones hurts. In ministry, losing launch team members is agonizing. Subtraction compels us to action. But subtraction is a normal part of life, including the life of a church. Think about the first 500 churches founded in the first century. None are still around today. All (100 percent) of the early churches ultimately experienced subtraction, all the way to their death. But the Church is still around and vibrant today. Not because of the growth of churches, but rather because of the *sending nature* of churches.

As hard as it is to accept and unless God changes the way He has worked in His church for 2,000 years, *any* church that experiences growth will ultimately experience subtraction. It's as certain as death. Churches are born and will eventually die (including yours). Subtraction is inevitable. Embrace it. The reality is that subtraction will likely be the final chapter in whatever church you lead (or start).

I know it's hard to imagine, but the largest and most influential churches in America, led by remarkable leaders like Rick Warren, Bill Hybels, Craig Groeschel and Andy Stanley, will experience the same fate as your church: subtraction leading to death. The only question is when. With the same Kingdom math that applies to your church, their legacies will ultimately be measured not by what they accumulated and kept, but rather by what they released and sent. It's the story of Christianity and the church.

Let that sink in. Don't let that reality discourage you, but do let it mess with your thinking. In all the turmoil of subtraction, we desperately pursue and seek out addition growth. But addition is temporary. It's multiplication that carries the legacy of your church to future generations and beyond the accumulation you achieve in your micro strategy.

That's why sending out leaders to multiply and start new churches and continue the movement into the future is so vitally important. Like today's most influential churches, your sending capacity might be your best asset, and your sending results could ultimately be your primary legacy.

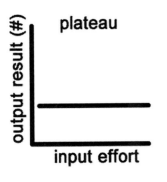

Plateau. When a church is plateaued, the # or output result remains steady over time. Each increment of input effort results in no discernable change in sustained output. Some behavioral experts would argue that most things do not remain plateaued over extended periods of time, but tend to be transitionary, meaning either subtraction or addition is likely to emerge from seasons of plateau. A leader of a church that is plateaued might often comment, *"We've been stuck for a few years, but we're working to regain momentum."*

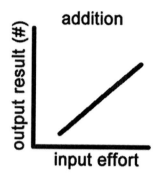

Addition. In the addition growth culture, the output result or number (#) increases with time. The addition line slants "up and to the right." With each incremental increase in input effort, you see a positive output result. For example, you might run a marketing campaign (input effort) and see more people show up on Sunday. Or maybe open a new building (input effort) and see new people show up on Sunday (output results). We instinctively want to see our effort produce fruit. For most of us, results are an inherent motivator. Like the graph shows, input effort fuels output results. To sustain growth, we must continually look for new and innovative ways to grow the output result through our input efforts. New programs, new buildings, cool community centers, great marketing campaigns, new sites, the best worship in town, etc., are all input fuel for output results.

Bill Hybels, founder and senior pastor of Willow Creek Community Church and the Global Leadership Summit, once told me that it gets harder and harder each year at the Leadership Summit to produce the same incremental increase in output quality. In other words, the "up and to the right curve" always wants to taper off to a lower level of output.

Output results become increasingly difficult unless you continually refresh your input efforts. It's not about working or trying harder but rather staying on the leading edge of innovation and creating an infrastructure to support the new directions. This propensity to live on the leading edge is largely responsible for the success of the megachurch movement. These churches have at least temporarily figured out how to stay on the leading edge of fresh, innovative input effort to keep feeding the output.

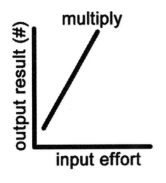

Multiplication. In the Multiplication culture, at first glance the multiply line might be confused for the addition line. In both addition and multiplication, output results increase with each incremental input effort. The difference is in the rate of the increase. Addition growth typically yields "fractional" output. In other words, each 1 unit of input effort yields less than or equal to 1 unit of output. For example, 1 increases to 1.1, then 1.2, 1.3 and so on. However, multiplication growth increases far more rapidly: 1 increases to 2 then to 4 then to 8 and so on. Multiplication produces a steeper rise in output for a given level of input. You might say that multiplication is "extreme or radical addition" (e.g., "and God added about 3,000 to their numbers that day"). You might also say the same level of input effort will give far greater output results in a multiplication growth culture.

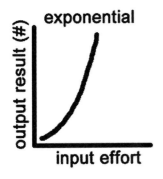

Exponential (Radical Multiplication) Notice that the output result in exponential multiplication is now increasingly disproportionate to the input effort applied. Unlike addition that needs to work harder on each successive cycle of input-output, exponential phenomena actually increase more with each cycle. Think about the idea of acceleration where an object just keeps increasing its rate of speed. You might describe "exponential" as exhibiting accelerating multiplication. In fact, our tagline at Exponential is "accelerating multiplication." Scientists describe exponential growth as a chain reaction (see the adjacent image) with increasing output on each successive cycle. If this picture continued on, it would take the shape of the exponential curve above.

33

Lets look at Ralph Moore's church again. From seven churches to 700+. You simply can't get there through addition. It takes multiplication moving toward radical multiplication. It takes a chain reaction.

Burn a picture of each of these curves in your mind:

- Subtraction characterized by decreasing numbers.
- Addition characterized by increasing numbers but at a relatively low, consistent level.
- Multiplication by more drastic increases.
- Radical or exponential multiplication like a chain reaction with ever-increasing outputs.

Clearly, we need to celebrate addition growth culture, as it is doing most of the heavy lifting of growth in the U.S. Church. But at the same time, we need to recognize that our story is missing the vital element of multiplication. As I talked about in chapter 1, we need our macro growth strategies to be focused on multiplication rather than addition.

Pause and think again about the culture you're creating. But this time, really press into the strategies, role models and methods that consume your time and thinking. Which culture are they really rooted in? Are you dwelling in a survival/subtraction culture, an addition culture, or a multiplication culture?

Let me ask the question differently. If God answered all your prayers today and solved the church tensions you face and struggles that get you down, which mathematical curve above would blossom into full bloom? Be honest. You probably want to say multiplication, but you can't. It's highly likely your paradigm of success is the best of the addition-growth paradigm. It's the scorecard we've embraced, and that has become part of our paradigm for success. Possibly without consciously knowing it, you've embraced an addition-growth scorecard for your measure of success.

Growth Barriers

Let look at the sustainability issue of addition compared with multiplication and radical multiplication. As we move from addition to multiplication to radical multiplication, the same level of input effort produces increasing results. You might say that multiplication (and especially exponential or radical multiplication) is far more efficient at producing output results than addition. It's the difference between a 12 MPG old car and an 80 MPG hybrid; for the same unit of input, we get far more output.

Let me introduce one last mathematical concept. (I promise it's the last one, and you can handle it). The concept will help tie a number of things together in contrasting addition growth with multiplication growth. In the previous graphs, the addition growth curve is a continually upward and to the right. However, that is not how addition growth naturally occurs in nature.

My conversation with Bill Hybels about the increasing effort it takes to produce the Global Leadership Summit is a good illustration. In nature, each successive cycle of input effort must work even harder to produce the same output result as the previous cycle. To maintain the same efficiency of output, we must continually innovate and come up with fresh inputs, essentially what Bill said to me. This physical phenomenon in nature is called "asymptotes."

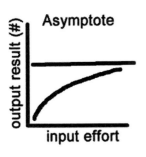

An "asymptote" is like a limit or barrier. In the graph, notice the start of the curve appears up and to the right like the addition curve in the previous graphs. However, with each additional input effort, the output appears to "slow" or become slightly less than the previous increment. As time and the associated input effort increases, the output results appear to become

35

constrained by and approach the asymptote. In nature, the "Asymptote" (represented by the horizontal line in the graph) physically acts like a buffer or limit to suppress the output.

In a church context, this physical phenomenon explains why church leaders and growth experts often say, "there are a number of well-known natural growth barriers at 120, 200, 500, 800, 2000, etc." In other words, what got us to where we are is not going to get us to where we need to go. To break the 500 barrier, we can't act like we did when we had 40 people. We need to change what we do to break through the current asymptote. Unfortunately, another asymptote a little higher up on the growth curve will be waiting for us.

This continual challenge and struggle to conquer the next hill or growth barrier can trap churches in a macro-addition strategy versus cultivating a macro-multiplication strategy. To break through these continual growth barrier challenges, releasing and sending resources to start new churches must be a priority. Functionally, our macro strategy becomes an addition-based strategy of breaking through the next growth barrier.

This progression of conquered hills is also leaving a growing number of pastors questioning whether they've "put their ladder against the right wall": What if we climb the ladder of addition-growth success only to realize someday we've had our ladder against the wrong wall? I still remember the first cohort of leaders in our Future Travelers initiative when Senior Pastor Steve Andrews said to the group, "I planted my church, and God grew it big. We've done externally focused, church planting, and multisite, and we'll keep doing them. But there are not enough years left in my life to simply keep growing this thing bigger. I'm interested in something more viral. I'm interested in changing the conversation from 'where is our next one?' to 'how do we release 250 of our members to take our city?'"

The seemingly endless sideways energy of each new barrier (asymptote) is causing these pastors to question whether the addition-growth culture we've created (and they've embraced) is really the right way. In essence, these pastors are realizing they need a macro-multiplication strategy rather than a macro-addition strategy.

Addition growth physically and naturally must contend with the principle of "asymptote." In reality, multiplication must deal with the same concept. However, when you get to radical or exponential multiplication, the rules change. In radically multiplying churches and movements, you see the following characteristics:

- Very simple, focused models and approaches that do not rely on continually changing strategies and input efforts

- An almost anti-asymptote phenomenon that many would use to describe the seemingly spontaneous expansion of the early Church. This phenomenon is at the heart of why radically multiplying churches would have to intentionally and deliberately try not to multiply. When you have an exponential model or framework, the asymptote essentially reverses itself and provides a "force" or pressure to keep the multiplication going.

The telling question we want to pose to both planters and leaders of established churches (regardless of context) comes down to what *type* of growth are you pursuing or experiencing? Addition or multiplication?

Consider this: Growth will always yield at least addition (and vice versa), but growth does not always produce multiplication. As a result, we can become satisfied with addition growth, but fall far short of experiencing multiplication growth. Our satisfaction with addition growth yields 20 percent of churches within its clutches with less than .005 percent fueled by radical multiplication.

Addition growth is good, but multiplication growth is even better.

In the way that growth is common to subtraction, addition, multiplication and radical multiplication, reproduction is common to these cultures, as well. We can reproduce and still lose ground. Population experts track, by country, what the "minimum reproduction rate per family" must be to sustain a population. If the average family reproduces at or below the minimum, the population will decline over time. And, like growth, reproduction finds its significance in its rate, not simply that it's happening. However, unlike growth, reproduction is a key source (or cause) of it.

Bottom line: A positive rate of growth and reproduction is important, but we should not be satisfied with less than multiplication.

Three Cultures, Lots of Tensions

Leadership consultant Dr. Samuel Chand goes so far as to say that a church's culture determines the actual direction of a ministry— even more than published vision or mission statements. "The strongest force in an organization is not vision or strategy—it is the culture which holds all the other components," Chand says. Or, as Peter Drucker is known for saying, "Culture eats strategy for breakfast."

In the previous series of graphs, we looked at what creates subtraction, addition and multiplication cultures (output results and input efforts), but let's drill down further to discover how these cultures are playing out in today's Church landscape.

Subtraction and Plateau - The vast majority of churches in the United States, as many as 80 to 90 percent, exist in a subtraction or survival culture. The average church in America plateaus below 100 members and struggles to grow. They are in survival mode, often experiencing subtraction. We talked about this earlier, but let me remind you of the characteristics of these churches. The lead pastor wants to be full time, and their top priorities are finances, starting with their own salary. It takes about 100 members to support a full-time pastor, so there is a constant and real tension on finances. They have a "scarcity" mentality with a perspective of, "We will add staff after we can afford it." Unfortunately until they grow, these churches can't seem to ever afford to do the things needed to springboard into addition culture. They are stuck.

Addition - The second culture to consider is addition-growth culture. Some 10 to 20 percent of U.S churches find themselves here. We've talked extensively in this chapter about our addiction for addition growth. In addition-growth churches, attendance is increasing and many are often externally focused, making an impact in their surrounding communities. Many churches have added multisite venues. In the midst of their growth, key tensions inevitably arise: How do we continue growing? How will we staff the ministries? How will we maintain the weekly production, mortgage and other associated costs of growth?

These churches have come face to face with growth tensions: Should we build? How much? What type? They've hired multiple staff. The pursuit of addition of staff has firmly established and rooted itself in the addition (micro)/addition (macro) orientation. Each new staff hire helps plug the existing hole or positioning for growth in an untapped area. Few of these leaders have ever been challenged with or even considered a different paradigm:

- Should we plant our first church before building?
- Should we plant our first church before doing our first site?
- Should we add a church planting intern/resident before our next staff hire?
- Should we tithe (give our first 10 percent) to church planting?

These leaders are at a crucial point in their development in terms of setting the course of their future relative to addition-growth culture versus multiplication-growth culture. There choices are numerous "line in the sand" decisions that could shape their core values, convictions and practices.

Multiplication - As I pointed out earlier, very few U.S. churches experience a multiplication culture. Exponential's dream and prayer is to see an increasing number of churches move into a radically multiplying (or exponential) culture—made up of less than .005 percent of U.S. churches. The leaders of these churches have planted hundreds of churches. They send hundreds of people to plant. Their scorecard is more about "who and how many have been sent" than "how many have been accumulated."

The Tipping Point

In his Exponential eBook, *Flow: Unleashing a River of Multiplication in Your Church, Community and World,* Larry Walkemeyer, pastor of Light & Life Christian Fellowship in Long Beach, California, and church planting pioneer, recalls this deeply personal shift from thinking addition to multiplication at the macro-strategy level:

"The vision was to stop becoming a *lake church* and instead become a *river church,*" he writes. "In a lake church, people flow in and stay. It seeks to get more and more people around one pastor in one place. In a river church, the people flow in but keep moving downstream. God takes them to other places to minister. The measurement becomes about 'flow rate' instead of 'volumes contained'; about 'gallons per minute' instead of 'gallons retained.'"

The culture that you create fuels whatever you value the most. If you're not careful, you will unintentionally create a culture that values subtraction/survival or addition and accumulation. Unless you're intentional about multiplication, you'll work hard to become the best lake church in town and miss the greater adventure of being a river church. In your zeal to grow, you may unintentionally neuter multiplication.

In describing what has happened in Ralph Moore's church, Ed Stetzer and Warren Bird conclude that multiplication is so deeply engrained in the church's DNA that Hope Chapel would have to try *not* to multiply. Let that be our prayer. May God let us cooperate and collaborate with Him in a way that multiplication becomes so engrained in who we are that we just can't stop it!

The challenge seems a bit daunting and unrealistic, doesn't it, especially when you consider Hope Chapel's trail of 700 churches! However, doesn't the radical multiplication of Hope Chapel and churches around the world characterize the movement nature of what we read about in the first-century Church—what Christ commissioned the Church to do?

When our conviction so perfectly lines up with our practices like what we read about in Acts, God's response is multiplication. It becomes the inevitable outcome. As a result, we pass a tipping point where our core conviction, our story and our practice are so strongly aligned with who we are that, like Stetzer and Bird say, we actually have to try *not* to multiply.

The two researchers pinpoint only one thing that needs to happen for church multiplication to become mainstream: "You need to do it!" they write. In other words, multiplication must be both a core conviction and part of your practice (for example, planting a church before buying a building; sending staff to plant; or supporting a church rather than keeping staff, etc.). At this point in your journey, do your practices as a leader and a church reflect what you say are your core convictions?

Aligning our convictions with our practices moves us toward the tipping point and positions us to ignite a culture of multiplication across the U.S. Church, ultimately fulfilling Jesus' Great Commission of disciple making.

So how do we get to this tipping point where we begin to see our churches shift from working hard to multiply to a place where reproduction is just a natural part of their DNA? How do we buck the norm and establish macro-level multiplication strategies and cultures rather than macro-level addition cultures?

Throughout the rest of this eBook and as the theme of Exponential 2015 we'll be talking about that question. Specifically, we'll focus on how we align our core convictions with our practice in such ways that over time we find ourselves sharing our own reproducing stories and reveling in the fruit of a culture of radical multiplication.

Chapter 3 - Foundations of a Powerfully Aligned Culture

They devoted themselves to the apostles' teaching and to fellowship, to the breaking of bread and to prayer. Everyone was filled with awe at the many wonders and signs performed by the apostles. All the believers were together and had everything in common. They sold property and possessions to give to anyone who had need. Every day they continued to meet together in the temple courts. They broke bread in their homes and ate together with glad and sincere hearts, praising God and enjoying the favor of all the people. And the Lord added to their number daily those who were being saved
(Acts 2:42-47).

When our conviction so perfectly lines up with our practices, like what we read about in Acts, God's response is growth. It becomes the inevitable outcome. As a result, we pass a tipping point where our core convictions, our stories and our practices are so strongly aligned with who we are that we actually have to try *not* to grow.

Pause and reflect on the culture we read about in Acts 2:42-47. What were their core values and convictions that shaped their stories and practices? Jesus, fellowship, prayer, and caring for one another.

Now think about the stories they sat and told one another. "Everyone was filled with awe" gives us a glimpse into the stories they were poised to tell. Imagine the power of the stories that started with, "I remember when Jesus ... ." The wonders and events this community of believers experienced in practice perfectly aligned with the teaching they received.

This combination resulted in two key outcomes that apply to most all strong cultures. First, "insiders," those who are part of the community or cause, become more fully devoted, raving fans of the cause. You might say they become owners in the crusade. The description in Acts uses the word "devoted." Devotion is the fuel of any movement. As people buy into the culture, devotion increases. Second, "outsiders," those not yet part of the community or cause, see what the insiders have and want it.

A powerfully aligned culture increases the devotion of insiders and fuels the addition of outsiders to join the cause. From Apple to Starbucks to your favorite local restaurant, every organization has a culture. You can't stop it. It's what you become known for, and it powerfully shapes the way you see the world and the decisions you make.

Try to picture yourself as part of that first-century band of believers described in Acts 2. These men and women had every reason to embrace a scarcity culture, and yet they lived out an abundance culture. We can learn from that.

Now read Acts 2 again, this time focusing on what you *don't* read. For many of us, the following is a better narrative of our experience:

> *They devoted themselves to vision clarity, optimized organizational structure, healthy teams, geographically based small groups, great preaching, monster outreach events, massive marketing campaigns, world- class children's ministry, the best music in town, leadership development, new sites, and the latest growth strategy to break the next barrier. Some of the believers came together weekly for an excellent Sunday morning show; others opted for overbooked schedules of travel sports and long work hours to pay increasing debt, leaving no margin for living in common. With a divorce, addiction and crime rate similar to society at large, outsiders simply mocked the church wondering why in the world they should be part of something so judgmental, hypocritical and irrelevant. Rather than praising God for the*

44

*abundance of blessing and being the fullness of
Christ in everything and in every way, they spent
their time praying for deliverance from the same
crazy, empty lives of their outsider friends. When
the numbers were not added daily, they looked for
the next silver bullet to catalyze the growth and
make the church more relevant. They desperately
sought to do church without being the church.*

Does this sound like the Acts church we study and continue to
learn from? Does it sound like our churches today? Each time I
present this to a church, I'm always amazed at how poignant (and
accurate) this description is.

As we discussed in the last chapter, your role in stewarding and
cultivating culture may be the most important role you play as a
leader. Value survival, and you'll establish a scarcity (subtraction)
culture. Value addition growth, and you'll establish an
accumulation culture. Value multiplication, and you'll establish a
sending culture.

In a recent article for *Forbes* magazine, Southwest Airlines
Founder Herb Kelleher says the unique core of any company's
success is the most difficult thing for others to imitate. Not their
products, services or unique strategies, but rather the distinctive
culture that penetrates and shapes everything they do. While
culture is notoriously difficult to define, leadership consultant
Samuel Chand says the best way to understand it is through the
statement: *This is how we do things here.* "Culture is the prevalent
attitude. It is the collage of spoken and unspoken messages," he
says.

Of course, for churches, building culture is vital for something far
more significant than profit or customer satisfaction. If we want to
see significantly more than 1 percent of U.S. churches radically
multiplying—a bona fide church planting movement in America—
we need to have powerfully aligned cultures like we see in the
Book of Acts.

How do you as a leader start to make the shift to a powerfully aligned culture that values and yields multiplication?

Elements that Shape Culture

Every culture regardless of its context shares these common elements: a unique and distinctive set of core values; a unique language and narrative that continually celebrates and communicates those values; and clear expectations, practices and behaviors that bring those values to life in tangible ways for people. People need to hear you say it in a way that makes sense and inspires action, and then see you doing what you say.

Each culture is unique and emerges from the burdens, passions and experiences God places in your heart. The most effective cultures powerfully align their core values, language and expected behaviors or practices in a manner that builds trust and devoted followers, and makes it simple for people to participate personally. When people easily get it and want to be part of it, your crusade or vision grows. Alignment of the pieces helps people know what you're about and that you are serious enough about it that your words translate to action and impact.

The model we're using for the basic elements of a powerfully aligned culture comes from leadership and culture consultant, Brian Zehr. Brian loves the church, works with numerous organizations and has experience working on staff helping lead a national church planting network.

In the diagram below, Zehr illustrates the importance of culture and how values, narrative and behaviors must align to form a powerful culture. Let's take a deeper look into each of these elements.

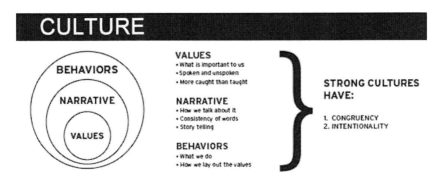

Values and Core Convictions

Zehr says that values can be discerned by asking the question: What is the most important thing we need to be doing or that we are about right now? What is important enough to us that it transcends all we do and shapes how we do what we do?

"I always say that if I go visit a church three or four weeks in a row, I can tell what's actually most important [to them]," Zehr says. "I can tell by how they interact with each other, by what things are prioritized and not prioritized in ministries. I can tell where mission is important or living on mission is important, or whether all they care about is themselves. I can tell whether they care about the community. So, more is caught from them than is actually taught."

Values are deeply embedded and shape how a local church does everything they do. You see it, you hear it and you feel it. Values are like a magnetic force field surrounding the people and operations of the church, proactively shaping the things to come and correcting the things that go off track. In the diagram above, values are shown as the center circle because they bring life, meaning and context to the other elements of narrative and behavior. The clarity of your narrative/language and your behavior/ practices is an overflow of the clarity and conviction of your values.

Prior to entering full-time ministry, I spent many years as an engineer at the U.S. Division of Naval Reactors. We were responsible for all aspects of nuclear propulsion in navy ships, including reactor and system design, operation, maintenance, repair and dismantling of reactor systems. The standards were stringent and the safety record unblemished. On the occasion of our 50th anniversary and in achieving over 100 million miles powered in nuclear ships, dignitaries from around the world sent their congratulations.

The vice president of the United States asked, "What is the secret of excellence in the Naval Reactors organization?" Without hesitation, our director said, "Excellence is a concept [value] so deeply engrained in whom we are that the word never needs to be used." I remember hearing that and thinking, *Wow, I don't remember ever hearing the word. I need to think about what it even means.*

Our record to outsiders shouted "excellence!" It's what we became known for based on the results we achieved. But we never sat around talking about excellence. Instead, we demonstrated excellence in everything we did—from the small things to the huge decisions. Excellence didn't happen overnight or through one act or decision, but emerged through the disciplined, consistent application of language and behaviors that were perfectly aligned to our core values.

Currently, the average person would not look at *Outreach* magazine's latest lists of the Top 100 largest and fastest-growing churches and ask, "What is the secret to your multiplication?" Instead they would ask questions like, "What is the secret to your growth?" or "What is the secret to your innovation?" or "How did you break the 500 growth barrier?"

As we discussed in chapter one, their questions would likely be rooted in the culture of addition growth they see in these churches. The questions outsiders ask from what they see, hear and experience give us the best insights into what our actual values are. Not what we want them to be, but what they really are.

Pause and reflect on the questions outsiders would most likely ask about your church. Be honest. What core values are bleeding through to the language and practices or behaviors that people see, feel and hear? Would they ask, "What is the secret to your multiplication?"

If not, go ahead and ask another really honest question: "How strong is your conviction to be a multiplying church?" Do you really want it, or is it just a nice concept? Are you willing to put to death the deeply embedded addition-growth paradigms that shape our definition of success in U.S. churches? Remember the story of Dan Smith and Momentum Christian Church in chapter one? Are you willing to declare, like Dan did, "As for me and my church, we will multiply from this day forward!"? If so, that story must start with multiplication becoming one of your most important core values.

Narratives

Let's revisit Southwest Airlines. To effectively reinforce their values, the company uses storytelling. Says Southwest CEO Gary Kelly: "Storytelling is the single most effective way to remind employees of the company's purpose and to reinforce the purpose in their day-to-day interactions with customers." To tell their story, every week Kelly gives a "shout out"—public praise—to employees who have gone above and beyond to show great customer service. And each month Southwest's *Spirit* magazine features the story of a deserving employee.

Our real core values shape and define our language and our narratives—*how* we talk about what matters most to us. This is why "outsiders" or visitors can discern so much about our true values in one visit to our churches.

If your church says one of your core values is caring about the surrounding community, then the language you're using to naturally describe that care should indicate your convictions. Do the people in your church talk about inclusiveness and building relationships in the community? Or is the conversation more about simply giving money to various community efforts? Do you integrate regular stories of community engagement and impact in your sermons, newsletters, printed materials, etc.?

Make this personal. In your life, you tend to talk about and get most excited about the things you care most about. It's the "twinkle in the eye" and "pep in the step" effect. These things shape your language and your practices. They most naturally reflect your passions or burdens. Our passion and burdens provide a direct lens into our values.

I have the privilege of working alongside Bob Buford, founder of Leadership Network (leadnet.org) and Halftime (halftime.org). For over 25 years, Bob was mentored by Peter Drucker, the father of modern management. Inevitably, in virtually every conversation Bob and I have, Peter Drucker's name comes up. Bob will lean forward with a twinkle in his eye, and newfound vibrancy in his voice and say, "I remember when Peter said ... ."

Bob is passionate about Peter's message of applied management, and you might say, "All paths for Bob find their way back to Peter." Bob can't help it. His core values and convictions naturally overflow to shape and define his language and narrative.

Pause and reflect on your church's language and narrative. Are there specific themes or patterns? What core values do the stories reflect? Are there core values you publicly state, but if you're honest don't have the stories to bring them to life?

Zehr offers this caution: "I remember when a church I was working with told me their key value was life-changing relationships with God. But when I asked to hear a recent story about someone whose life was changed, leaders could only recall stories from decades ago. This church was either suffering from wishful values, or not living out their values."

There is also real danger in forcing language and storytelling that doesn't line up with our real core values. In our zeal to be or project something that we're not, we risk being perceived as disingenuous or shallow. People will see through and pick up on the integrity of how what we say (or don't say) lines up with what we do (or don't do).

Language and narrative (storytelling) are a powerful bridge between our core values and our practices. Ultimately, all organizations share the common goal of continually increasing the number of people who join and participate in their unique crusade. Our language and narrative are key components in helping move people from *knowing* our core values (the first element of culture discussed above) to actively *participating* in what we do (the third element of culture discussed below).

Several years ago, I read Andy Stanley's book, *Seven Practices of Effective Ministry*. At its core, the book is about strategic planning and thinking. Interestingly, I'm not sure the book ever uses the word "strategic" and yet is one of the best church books I've ever read on strategic thinking and alignment. Why? I'm guessing Stanley deliberately avoided a language that makes most pastors glossy-eyed. Which book would you prefer to read: one on strategic planning in the design of your core systems and processes, or a book on how to more effectively align your culture to move people from "disconnected" to fully devoted followers of Jesus?" Same book but different language/narrative. It makes all the difference in connecting with the audience.

Over six years later, I can distinctly remember my core learnings from the book (and very few books do that for me). To explain how increasing relational intimacy helps people move along a growth continuum, Stanley uses a metaphor: from "the foyer, to the living room, to the kitchen." Here's the summary (note the language and storytelling):

"People we don't know come to our door and experience our foyer. It's safe for them, and they get a glimpse into our home. The conversations in the living room are more intimate but still safe. We know the people who make it to our living room, but not necessarily intimately. They have elected to be there, typically by invitation. Those who make it to our living room learn more about us and what makes us tick, but are still "safe" in what they share. Finally, a few people who have living room privileges also make it to the kitchen table. The conversations in the kitchen are intimate and press into the deeper issues of life. We are most vulnerable in the kitchen, but also best positioned for transformative growth."

One metaphor—different rooms or environments in our homes—and three sets of words (foyer, living room and kitchen) create a powerful vocabulary familiar to both insiders and outsiders, and memorable. As you'll see in the section below, this language can then powerfully align with the actions we want both insiders and outsiders to take (the behaviors and practices we seek). When this happens, we have a powerfully aligned culture. The language and narrative serve as a bridge.

All three elements of culture must work synergistically to amplify and enhance one another. Once our core values and language are aligned, then we have to ensure our practices and behaviors also line up.

Behaviors, Practices and Decisions

The third element of culture is where you might say, "the rubber meets the road." You can have perfect values and a great narrative, but if your behaviors and practices are inconsistent with the story you tell, you'll struggle. Your behaviors and practices will always be self-correcting and align to your *real* values and story.

You can have the most fancy statements on the wall and tell the best story in town, but if your actions tell a different story, you lose credibility. And credibility and trust help fuel causes.

52

Our words and thinking can say that we are a lean, fit and healthy athlete. But the food we eat, the weight that displays on the scale, and the blood pressure reading tell the real story. The results and outcomes, and the behaviors that produce them, are the proof of our real values. They tell the real, truthful story.

To increase the alignment of our culture, we can do three key things to align our actions (and decisions) with our story and narrative:

- *Intentionality and discipline* - Deliberately pause at some frequency and assess whether the things you're doing are congruent with the values you espouse and the narrative you tell. Then proactively look for and find stories, metaphors and language that reinforce whom you want to be. We need to exercise care and discipline when telling stories or using language that could appear inconsistent with our values and actions.

  For example, if you value personal evangelism, be careful about how you celebrate the results of direct mail marketing campaigns. Rather than celebrating the impersonal activity or action of direct mail and the resulting new people showing up at church, find and celebrate stories of church members who used the direct mail card to invite their neighbor to church. Same action, but different narrative.

  Most churches are disciplined at creating a sermon schedule for the coming months. Consider creating a similar matrix/schedule of powerful stories that bring to life how your core values are being lived out into action.

- *Aligning the desired actions we want people to take (and processes that facilitate them) with our core values and language* - Look again at Stanley's house metaphor and Dan Smith's sending scorecard. In both cases, the language and narratives help the "outsider" who experiences your church and becomes an "insider," to easily take ownership of the process and then bring other outsiders along in the journey. The cycle easily repeats when the language and the practices are tightly integrated.

When people attending Momentum Christian Church continually hear about the scorecard of sending, they naturally begin to ask themselves what it will look like for them to be sent. The language and practices naturally help people to transition from "if" to "when" as they take ownership for the cause.

In Stanley's house metaphor, "foyer, living room and kitchen" environments and what happens in those environments become a powerful shaping factor of what you do (example, types of events and activities) and how you do them. To this day, when church staff members are thinking about starting a new program or activity, I continue to ask, "Is that a foyer, living room or kitchen activity?" and "How will that help move people to the next environment?"

We must seek to powerfully and simply link the language and narrative we use with the behaviors and actions we want people to take. And that process must be simple. From our initial review of multiplication-growth cultures, it appears they tend to be far more simple and reproducible than the addition-growth strategies that are always reliant on the next leading-edge idea or innovation.

- *Micro/macro (addition and multiplication) integration* - In chapter one, we introduced the idea of having a synergistic "micro" and "macro" strategy. The "micro" strategy is unapologetically addition-oriented: "Where is the next one?" It's the most basic behavior for members impacting non-members. It's the core fuel of the crusade. In addition-growth culture, the "macro" strategy is also addition-oriented. Multiplication-growth culture distinguishes itself with multiplication at the "macro" level. You must also ensure that there is a congruency and synergy between the micro and macro strategies. When the micro results naturally feed and fuel the required macro inputs, we experience better results. In other words, the micro is either feeding the macro, or it's competing with it.

Let's expand on the house metaphor. The "foyer, living room and kitchen" are a powerful "micro" strategy for adding the next one. The rooms (environments) are vitally important to the process. But don't miss the most important environment. Growth within a house is naturally constrained to the rooms in that house. Multiplication occurs when the house replicates itself from one to two to four to 100 new houses.

In this expanded metaphor, the micro-strategy is the "foyer, living room and kitchen," and the macro-strategy is the building of new houses (each of which becomes the incubator of more rooms/environments at the micro-level).

In the absence of new houses at the macro-strategy level, what options does a church have for continuing to expand its growth? It either builds more facilities and adds more staff to handle the new rooms in the existing house; or it starts new sites with new staff to expand capacity. Both are solid strategies but if we're not careful they easily lead to dead ends in multiplication. Both approaches or strategies are subject to the "asymptote" principle we discussed in chapter two, and rarely do you see facilities or sites that replicate themselves with the same aggressiveness as the parent campus.

In other words, we add facilities and sites to add growth, but rarely do we the scenario in which these added facilities or sites become incubators for multiplication. You might say their primary role is in expanding micro-strategy capacity at the local level. The problem arises when we adopt multisite as a macro-addition strategy in lieu of a multiplication-based macro strategy.

Defining Questions and Decisions

Most of our tensions and the resulting practices we put in place in response to them find their roots in a handful of key questions. They are the types of questions all leaders face in seeking to grow their churches, and these questions play a vital role in shaping the culture they create.

Brett Andrews faced many of these tensions. He was called to plant a church in Chantilly, Virginia (New Life Christian Church). Like many of you, he started with just his wife and practically no money or expertise. He had more questions than answers, but did have a conviction to lead a church planting church that would be faithful with the little under its care—trusting that God would bless with even more.

Brett had no idea what it meant or would take to be a church planting church. But again, he had passion and conviction. After three years of struggle in the survival culture, New Life took a deep breath and celebrated being financially self-sufficient. The journey was not easy. Brett tells of the seasons when he was unsure whether anyone would show up the next week, or whether his family would have money for food. Like most planters, he lost some of his closest friends who left the launch team. So that deep breath of celebration came at a deep cost and within the context of struggle.

But also with that deep breath came a number of defining moments: "Would we buy land and build? Or plant our first church? Would we take care of our own internal family's needs to care for the 99 safe sheep? Or would we risk everything and go after the one lost sheep? Would we let go and send our best staff? Or hold on to them tightly?"

To plant their first church, New Life chose to release two of their three staff members and a significant portion of their budget, rather than follow the conventional path to build a facility. After all, facilities help legitimize your existence. In retrospect, that one decision set the course for who New Life would become. From that point on, the church has gone on to be involved in more than 100 church plants, has founded several church planting support ministries, and even helped start Exponential.

There is a good chance you've never heard of Brett. The scorecards of multiplying churches don't land you on the Top 100 lists. But pause and imagine the impact of New Life not making that one decision. Had they waited until the elusive day when the resources lined up correctly to plant churches, their impact would now be measured primarily by their addition rather than their multiplication.

Remember Dan Smith's story from the introduction—100+ leaders sent to plant or be part of planting teams. Dan is a church planter out of Brett's church. Where would those 100+ leaders be now if Brett had chosen to build a building rather than plant their first church? The chain reaction of multiplication is profound.

Bottom line is that we can't establish a multiplication growth culture without bucking conventional thinking and making some radical decisions. How prepared are you? Are you willing to:

- Plant your first church before building or buying your first building;

- Send your first church planter before accumulating your first two to three staff members;

- Commit the first fruits of your financial resources, tithing 10 percent or more to church planting, even before paying other essentials like salaries;

- Plant your first church before starting your first multisite;

- Come alongside and coach other church planters in your area who can benefit from your encouragement and experience;

- Start or join a church planting network, locally or nationally, to collaborate with others, find accountability for multiplying and building a multiplication culture, and get involved in more than you otherwise could?

Moving Forward

Knowing how culture is created and nurtured allows us to look ahead to the predictable tensions that you will inevitably face in putting a multiplication growth culture in place. For example, if your church commits to a $6 million building campaign before it plants a church, what does that say about your priorities? Or if you call yourself a multiplying leader, but continue adding more staff before you train and release a church planter, what are you modeling for your church?

Most of these key decisions draw defining boundaries around the specific culture you create: The beautiful new building we want will give us momentum and accelerate growth. The best staff members will help us break the next growth barrier. The new site will help us expand the number of services we offer.

These decisions are the right ones for addition growth and certainly enhance our micro- growth strategies for reaching the "next one." But we simply need to understand that those decisions can also become the barriers that keep us from creating a multiplication culture and the right macro-level strategies. Remember, our actions define our real values. The best spin or marketing campaign in the world can't change that.

Our tensions will often call leaders to take holy risks. If you feel called to build a multiplication culture in your church, no doubt you'll face the "Kingdom math" tension. It's not a question of whether you will grow your church. Growth is good. The profoundly more important question is whether it is through addition growth or multiplication growth.

Exponential President and New Thing Network founder Dave Ferguson notes that one of the biggest tensions we face centers around sacrifice and surrender. As a leader, one of the most difficult (and rewarding) tasks is to raise up and train other leaders. In a multiplying church, the tension will surface: Do we send out these leaders, those we've invested in so much and who are doing great ministry? Or do we hang on to them? Our actions speak loudly and trump our narrative.

In the next chapter, we'll highlight the most common types of tensions you'll face in seeking to move beyond addition thinking to multiplication thinking. In each of our subsequent eBooks in the "SPARK" series, local church practioners will candidly share with you how they've experienced and dealt with these tensions. Be prepared. This is a dangerous journey and will require you to put to death some of the things you've grown to idolize. Overcoming these tensions will take courage, persistence and intentionality.

Spark: Igniting a Culture of Multiplication

Chapter 4 - Tensions and Troubles: Culture Shapers

"Five times I received from the Jews the forty lashes minus one. Three times I was beaten with rods, once I was pelted with stones, three times I was shipwrecked, I spent a night and a day in the open sea, I have been constantly on the move. I have been in danger from rivers, in danger from bandits, in danger from my fellow Jews, in danger from Gentiles; in danger in the city, in danger in the country, in danger at sea; and in danger from false believers. I have labored and toiled and have often gone without sleep; I have known hunger and thirst and have often gone without food; I have been cold and naked. Besides everything else, I face daily the pressure of my concern for all the churches" (2 Cor. 11:24-28).

~ Paul, church leader and planter

Amidst their growth, the early Christians experienced difficulty. The Apostle Paul reminds us of his ongoing tensions and troubles, but also notes that our trials are but momentary compared with the reward that awaits us.

In his last days before going to the cross, Jesus said to His disciples, "In this world, you will have trouble. But take heart! I have overcome the world" (John 16:33). In His subsequent series of prayers, Jesus asked His Father to protect the disciples amidst their troubles. Watch closely for what He did and did not ask: "My prayer is not that you take them out of the world but that you protect them from the evil one" (John 17:15).

In other words, Jesus said, "My prayer is not that you take away their troubles, but instead protect them from the evil one, and the mind games he will play when their troubles come."

It's not a matter of "if," but rather "when." In Eph. 6:13, Paul says, "Put on the full armor of God, so that when the day of evil comes, you may be able to stand your ground." Again, not "if" but "when" the day of trouble comes.

Wouldn't it be so much easier if Jesus had asked God to take away the trouble rather than letting adversity be a normal part of Christianity? Wouldn't it be so much easier to recruit followers to our cause with the promise of a "trouble-free life?" Jesus could've made the path level and easy (or even downhill) for us.

There must be something about the trouble and tension we face in this life that's important to our journey toward heaven. In fact, trouble and tension helped shape the culture of the early Church and those who were a part of it just as it can help shape our lives and our churches today.

First, our tensions and troubles point us to God. We can't start and grow churches in our own strength. In describing his own tensions, Paul said, "We were under great pressure, far beyond our ability to endure, so that we despaired of life itself. Indeed, we felt we had received the sentence of death. But this happened that we might not rely on ourselves but on God, who raises the dead" (2 Cor. 1:8-10). Jesus said that He would build *His* church, not our churches. Our tensions need to keep pointing us back to Jesus, His ways, and what He would have us do. As we discussed in chapter one, His ways point us to the genius of the *and*: addition growth (adding and making disciples at the micro or local church level) and multiplication growth (macro or sending disciples to start new communities of faith).

Second, tensions and troubles naturally foster a culture of "gathering *and* scattering" (the micro and macro we've discussed). Troubles often lead us to the safety and security of community, and gathering together with like-minded family—the fellowship of believers described in Acts 2. As outsiders see the way insiders share and care for one another amid their struggles, they want the elusive thing the insiders have. The "gathering" becomes the most effective evangelism we have. Our tensions and troubles, and the way we live through them, should help build a stronger "gathering" culture in which disciples are made, and that helps attract and grow the next "one."

Trouble also quite literally "scattered" the early church to *go*. Jesus commanded us to go and make disciples. Persecution gave the *go* extra momentum (or a springboard start). We see the *go* impulse more visibly in international movements, often where persecution of Christians exists. In the absence of persecution in the United States, it becomes important for us to be intentional about putting cultures in place that will naturally propel and springboard the *go* or *sending* impulse. We need a solid multiplication strategy of sending to complement our local church strategy for adding and making disciples.

As we've seen in the previous chapters, if we're not deliberate, the "gather" growth, and the energy to sustain it, will naturally overtake the "scatter" impulse. The resources to "scatter" or *go* feel like they are in conflict with the resources needed to stay and grow. The rest of this chapter focuses on the specific tensions that can keep us from being intentional in the sending strategies that position us for multiplication.

Igniting a healthy culture of multiplication in your church will be messy. As any multiplying leader can tell you, the path is full of tensions. Some of the very things that move leaders from subtraction to addition are also the very things that pull them back from moving into multiplication. The reality is that building a culture of multiplication will often mean "un-learning" the values, narratives and behaviors that might have built a successful addition culture church.

Exponential President Dave Ferguson challenges leaders: "You have to be personally engaged if you really want to see your culture shift." That means creating an infrastructure of movement and reproduction, along with a willingness not only to train, build and invest in leaders, but also to send and release them.

Internal Tensions

Let's start in our own hearts. Prov. 4:23 says, "Above all else, guard your heart, for everything you do flows from it." God said through the prophet Jeremiah, "I the Lord search the heart and examine the mind." Clearly, God cares more about the condition of our hearts than He does our accomplishments. If we seek to make wise decisions to influence our external actions, we should first look hard at the internal tensions that shed light on the motives of our heart. In the words of King David in Psalm 26:2, let this be our prayer: "Test me, Lord, and try me, examine my heart and my mind."

How we handle and deal with our internal tensions makes all the difference in how we deal with the external tensions and realities of growing our churches. Do we have the right motives and personal scorecards?

Larry Walkemeyer, pastor of Light & Life Fellowship in Long Beach, California, described to me the personal process he went through to move his church in the direction of a multiplication culture.

"It had to start in my own heart," he said. "I had to do a tough and candid assessment of the scorecard that was motivating me to produce results. God had to do a work in me before He could do a work through me. During that process, He revealed a number of things that needed to change in me to enable the changes that were needed in my church."

Larry shared a number of the things he processed in his own life. Don't be overwhelmed by this list. Instead, use it as a diagnostic tool to assess the condition of your heart as it relates to your approach to church growth. You may have additional internal tensions, but this is a good starting place for self-assessment. Also, this is not a pass-fail test. We all have struggles that hold us back from being all that God wants us to be. Simply use this list to let God reveal in you things you either need to change or need to be on guard for.

- **Ego:** Is your personal self-image predicated on the size of your church?

- **Pride**: Do you consider the church "yours" instead of "His"? Does anything that threatens the image of the church threaten your self-image, too?

- **Fear:** Do you fear failure at your church planting attempts? Do you fear that "mother church" will be unduly impacted by the attempt?

- **Unbelief:** In practice, do you live as though your church's success has more to do with you than with God? Do you find it difficult to trust God to replenish what you give away? Deep down, do you believe it's more blessed to receive than to give?

- **Complacency:** Are you willing to work hard to not only tend to your own flock but also help another church start? The hard work required often diminishes the motivation of multiplication.

- **Competition:** Is your scorecard for success based on "bodies, budgets and buildings"? Does your zeal to obtain these 3 B's block your ability to prioritize multiplication?

- **Comparison:** Do you measure your ability to multiply by your evaluation of other leaders or churches you've watched do it so successfully? Ever say to yourself, *I'm not as good as they are*? Have you seen a church planting failure and thought *that will inevitably happen to me, as well*?

- **Harmony:** Deep down, do you think the battle to sell such a radical vision is worth the fight? Does significant pushback or division tempt you to truncate the vision to a more self-serving initiative?

- **Ignorance:** Have you been adequately exposed to a multiplication vision or the information you need to instill a priority of a multiplication culture?

- **Celebrity tunnel vision:** Are your heroes addition-growth culture pastors? Are they the people you learn from and seek most to emulate even though they don't lead multiplication?

- **Denominational prestige:** Do you seek out your denomination's award or recognition based on attendance and dollars with little regard for multiplication?

- **Control:** Do you desire to multiply ministries even though you'll have no direct control over them? Does your reluctance to relinquish control restrict multiplication?

- **Fastidiousness:** In many aspects, church planting is usually messy and non-linear. Does that create an insurmountable internal issue for you?

- **Restrictive models:** Have you only seen church planting modeled in certain (usually, financially costly) ways that automatically preclude you from envisioning a culture of multiplication?

- **Demonic resistance:** Satan hates church planting and will lie in every way to undermine and resist the church leader who pursues such a Kingdom mission.

External Tensions

Usually, reaching a tipping point doesn't happen all at once, or simply because a senior leader issues a vision statement from the front. In his watershed book, *The Tipping Point*, author Malcolm Gladwell reminds us, "That is the paradox of the epidemic: that in order to create one contagious movement, you often have to create many small movements first." Over the next few pages, we introduce 18 of the tensions you'll likely encounter in growing a church. Many of these tensions are interconnected and will overlap at different points.

These tensions are based on the experiences of leaders and churches here in the United States. In Exponential's upcoming series of free eBooks, you'll hear from leaders of U.S. churches, as well as international churches and movements, city movements and new churches that are planting other churches. These leaders will share candidly with you the tensions they've faced, including the ones listed below. In providing this list, we are simply offering context for the eBooks to come; a framework of sorts for the eBook authors to share their tensions with you, including how they've dealt with them.

Navigating these tensions is a difficult journey, but is vital in shifting your church's culture, one decision at a time.

As you read through and consider these tensions, know that we are intentionally communicating them as "or" tensions to highlight the extremes of each end of the tension. However, in most cases we need to pursue the genius of the "and," especially as it relates to the balance and synergy between your micro (adding disciples through the local church) and macro (sending/multiplying disciples to start new churches).

A few things to keep in mind:

• **Our default path** - Know that our default path when struggling in the trenches of church work is the path of addition growth. Balancing the *and* is important because the "micro- strategy" (where is the next one?) and the "macro-strategy" (how do we reach the next 100,000?) must be synergistic. We need addition *and* multiplication.

• **Think "steward," not "owner"** - Before each airplane flight, the flight attendant makes a point of saying that in the event of an emergency if you're traveling with a young child to locate and secure your own breathing device before attending to your child. Good, sound, parental guidance. The best way to protect the life and health of the child is to first guarantee the life and health of the parent.

For many church leaders, this principle illustrates their approach to multiplication. Unfortunately, the elusive day of health and abundance never seems to arrive. There is always another next hill to conquer and growth barrier to break. Each hill brings new challenges to the health and vibrancy of the parent. However, when we're talking about a culture of multiplication and the decisions we must make as planting parents, it's vitally important that we assume the role of "steward" rather than "owner" of our churches. Allowing Jesus to be the owner, founder and "parent" empowers us to birth new churches where we might otherwise wait.

The list of tensions over the next few pages was developed in partnership with Larry Walkemeyer. Throughout the rest of Exponential's eBooks series, you'll find numerous leaders, including Larry, sharing their stories of how they have navigated some of these same tensions. As you read through these tensions, do your best to put on the hat of "steward of God's church" and not "owner of your church."

Tension #1: Here or There (Addition or Multiplication)
Should we focus on growing our attendance, or starting new places of growth?

In many ways, the most obvious metric for success for churches has been the number of people in attendance. Larger attendance numbers mean a bigger platform, which means more resources, perceived flexibility and perceived influence. Addition-growth churches prioritize their energy, money, talent, volunteers and leaders to help grow attendance. The primary lens of decision-making centers on building bigger and bigger churches. If you're going to guide your church into a culture of multiplication, you'll need to cast a vision to measure success differently. We need a "here *and* there" approach. In the previous chapters, we described this as a "micro-strategy" focused on addition-growth locally and a "macro-strategy" focused on multiplication beyond our context.

Light & Life Fellowship's Walkemeyer suggests relearning "Kingdom math" to guide this shift: "Addition is adept at bringing glory to God and to us; multiplication requires humility lived out," he writes in his upcoming Exponential eBook, *Flow: Unleashing a River of Multiplication in Your Church, Community and World.* "Multiplication demonstrates an 'it's not about us' dimension to ministry. It builds a different scoreboard—one that lights up when new leaders are sent out instead of simply when new consumers come in. The glory of the local church gets lost in the glory of the Kingdom."

While the number of people attending weekend services is a valid metric, especially in our micro-strategies for reaching "the next one," building a culture of multiplication means talking about success differently. Author and pastor Rick Warren says it well: "I'd rather see a church that's starting 10 churches than a church of 1,000 that is not." Fortunately, we don't have to choose one option over the other. The Church is designed to deliver both. We simply need to cooperate in that design.

Tension #2: Facility Acquisition vs. Facility Sacrifice
Should we focus on a church building that will establish us in the community, or invest those resources in planting?

Apart from the metric of attendance, people often look to structures as an important measurement of success. Often, when people talk about "church," they're referencing buildings and structures rather than the people who make up that church community. Again, there is great temptation to fall for this simple rule of thumb: A bigger church facility is directly proportional to greater success. We've bought into the 1980s film *Field of Dreams* message—"If you build it, they will come."

Dave Ferguson tells the story of Community Christian Church's first newcomers' reception. After sharing the heart and vision behind their new church, someone in the back of the room raised his hand and asked what was a significant question to Ferguson: "So when are you going to build a church building?"

"Leaders who want to radically multiply must create stories of movement before talking about land or buildings," Ferguson says.

Churches that build on actual values of planting and multiplication will sacrifice—willingly and joyfully—some of their comfort (for example, a permanent church facility, new carpet or air conditioning, the latest technical gear, etc.) for the sake of multiplying the Kingdom. This kind of atypical sacrifice can be jarring in our consumer culture. However, we believe that embracing this countercultural value will help point your church toward radical multiplication.

As we talked about at the end of chapter 2, a decision to build or buy a building, or add to an existing one, before planting your first church may lock you into an addition-growth culture that becomes increasingly more difficult to overcome.

Tension #3: Financial Security vs. Financial Uncertainty
Should we prioritize our financial stability or, in an act of faith, commit our financial resources to planting?

In his book, *Overrated: Are We More in Love with the Idea of Changing the World Than Actually Changing the World?*, church planter and thought leader Eugene Cho shares this compelling insight about followers of Jesus who engage in the work of justice: "I love justice. Justice is cool. Justice is glamorous ... It makes me feel heroic. I believe that most people—particularly followers of Jesus—love justice. Right? ... until there's a cost. But here's the tension and truth: There's always a cost to doing justice. And there's always a cost to following Jesus."

Jesus tells us in Luke 14 that His disciples will need to count the cost of following Him. For churches that want to ignite a culture of multiplication, very real costs and risks are involved—particularly in a financial sense. As the idea of multiplication takes root in your church's imagination and value systems, you'll need to be prepared not only to love the idea but also navigate these financial tensions.

People will naturally want to know the return on investment in planting new churches. Staff and other leaders will wonder how prioritizing your church's financial resources toward multiplication will impact their current ministries. It will be easy for many of your leaders to show that investing the resources into existing ministries or starting new sites is better stewardship. Still, others might suggest reaching specific financial goals before committing resources to planting. Without a strong core conviction to multiply, you *will* succumb to the addition-growth culture pathways.

Drawing from leadership consultant Brian Zehr's experience, many churches want to move to radical or exponential multiplication, but hit a roadblock when they realize the cost involved. Sometimes, even gathering leaders and resources for new ministries only further entrenches a culture of addition if the actual culture isn't changing toward multiplication.

Walkemeyer reminds us: "The reality is God is bigger than the X. God is not limited to our savings account. Jesus taught us to lay up our treasures above, not on earth. He wasn't denigrating savings accounts, but He was establishing priorities. Our security is not in more X number of dollars but in the ability of God and in His promises to those who follow His Kingdom priorities. We can trust the Almighty or the Dollar, but not both."

Tension #4: Attractional vs. 'Activational'
Should we try to draw more people by offering more comfort and better programs? Or challenge them to live sacrificially on mission with God?

"Have it your way" is more than a slogan for a fast food chain; it's a way of life in our consumer culture. In the push to grow ever-larger churches, addition culture can overemphasize the needs and desires of potential church members. Most often, the churches that grow the most provide the highest-quality religious goods and services.

However, that attractional impulse to draw in and retain is directly opposite to creating a culture of releasing, sending and multiplication. Attractional priorities in church ministry look for activities that reinforce attachment to the local church. Conversely, "activational" priorities challenge believers to do what is difficult—to avoid growing too attached to the amenities of the mother church but instead seek ways to engage in the mission of multiplication.

Our temptation is to cater to the consumers who will fund their own comfort instead of calling out the missionaries who will commit to building the Kingdom. The reality is that most churches are planted into survival (subtraction) culture, simply trying to build up enough members and resources to become self-sustaining. As we discussed earlier, the desperation of survival in those early days can lead to a strong impulse in the attractional activities that fuel addition growth. Those early days of building culture are naturally drawn to addition-growth paradigms, and these roots become increasingly difficult to pull up as the church gets older.

Zehr recommends conducting high-level leader meetings from the beginning, consistently reinforcing key values such as reproduction and evangelism. Avoid the mistake of starting out by focusing on the services your church can provide and then trying to shift to a multiplication culture a few years down the road. Even when churches conduct classes for new Christians, Zehr urges them not only to focus on how individual believers can grow, but also on how they can be a part of what God is doing in the world.

Tension #5: Filling Our Church vs. Starting A New Church
Should we focus on reaching a certain attendance goal before starting a new church, or begin planting regardless?

If you champion radical multiplication, make no mistake, you *will* face the tension of having empty space in the mother church that needs to be filled before considering starting a new church. You'll likely hear: "Why start something new when what we have is not full? Why not focus energy on this objective instead of dissipating energy by launching a new church?" Until the seats are full at multiple services at the mother church, there will be great temptation to delay planting.

The reality, though, is that there is no perfect set of conditions (attendance, finances, staffing, etc.) that will guarantee success for either the mother church or the plant. To move toward a radical multiplication culture, you'll need to recognize the remnant of addition culture that thinks attendance growth is the foundational key to success in planting.

Tension #6: New Campus vs. New Plant
Should we start a multisite campus, or plant a new church?

Facing this tension requires some soul searching and hard questions about what model of multisite you plan to implement, as well as your ultimate goal in starting a new campus. If the new campus is, in reality, simply overflow rooms that further showcase or deploy your gifts, then know you're likely acting from an addition-growth paradigm.

However, if your church is considering a new multisite location as a means to leverage the strength of the mother church whose goals include raising up new teaching; developing new indigenous leadership; creating new vision that addresses location-specific needs; *and* eventually starting a site or plant itself, then your church may be bucking the norm and innovating an approach that is more characteristic of multiplication.

Be aware that the energy you and your church expend to start and maintain a multisite campus can quickly drain the energy and resources for multiplying new churches. Multisite strategy can easily inhibit true multiplication, but it also can be an accelerator of it. As we talked about in chapter 2, multisite is a "macro strategy" of addition for most churches that do it. With a micro and macro strategy rooted in addition, these churches lock into an addition-growth culture.

The innovative churches of the future will demonstrate how to leverage multisite as a "macro strategy" of multiplication. To discern the difference, simply look at the numbers. Is each new site positioned, equipped and expected to reproduce into additional new sites from their context in the same way the mother or original campus does with its new sites? In other words, is each new site simply just new services created to extend the reach of the mother campus? Or is each new site expected to replicate additional sites the way the mother campus does?

Tension #7: Senior Leader Coasting vs. Senior Leader Climbing
Should I build systems that allow me to coast, or continue to ride uphill?

Navigating this tension requires you to honestly assess your personal energy and resiliency. Church planting can feel like riding a bicycle uphill. Then, just when you're about to crest the hill and coast for a season, you choose to turn right and start up a new hill. Most leaders find themselves focused on leveraging their energy to build a system, allowing them then to decrease their energy investment as they and their organization mature. Few leaders want to keep making multiplication choices that require increased leadership energy. Leaders who grasp the Kingdom value of building multiplication cultures in their churches rise up to meet these uphill challenges.

Tension #8: Staffing the Mother Church vs. Staffing the Plants
Should we hang on to our best staff members, or send them out as church planters?

Leadership development, Dave Ferguson points out, is a significant and difficult task, in and of itself. But to then take the step of sending out those flourishing leaders as planters—men and women in whom you've invested significant time and resources—is an even more difficult decision and undertaking. The same leaders who most effectively grow their micro-strategies for reaching "the next one" are also the leaders best suited to be sent. To say this creates tension would be a gross understatement.

Multiplication is a disruptive force for the mother church, requiring ongoing recruiting and training of new staff. It results in far more disruption and turnover than the safety of addition. This energy-consuming reality can also affect staff quality and unity. The commitment to launch your best staff is a steep—and also Kingdom-building—price for mother church to pay.

This tension is at the heart of the emergence of a growing number of intern and residency programs for church planters. Multiplying churches realize that leadership development and a solid pipeline of leaders are essential.

Tension #9: Mother's Maturity vs. Baby's Birth
Should we wait until we're mature enough to plant a church, or begin moving forward now in planting?

Churches who want to plant other churches are wise to want to replicate spiritually mature and healthy cultures. If you have massive dysfunction in the mother church, then it may make sense to put any planting plans on hold. The question is, how mature must a church be before giving birth to a new church?

Naturally, leaders seek a sense of security before taking a risk in planting. They might assemble committees, commission studies or hire consultants to learn to plant most effectively. However, avoid "paralysis by analysis."

Walkemeyer points out: "Most churches are waiting too long to give birth. They fail to see that reproduction can be a means to maturity. There is nothing like becoming a parent to make you ready to be a parent. The most effective personal evangelists are not those who are fully trained and matured but rather, those who are newly saved. The same is true for multiplication. The younger and fresher a church is, the more apt it is to start another one. As churches age, they tend to become more averse to the adventures of multiplication."

Tension #10: Volunteer Talent Retention vs. Release
Should we hang on to our best volunteers, or send them out as church planters or part of a launch team?

In addition-growth culture, the demands of creating excellent programs to attract as many people as possible require retaining as many volunteer leaders as possible. Radically multiplying churches raise up leaders with a view toward releasing them into church plants versus retaining them long-term to build your bench. In rapidly multiplying churches, the "leaders bench" might run less deep than they'd like because they're sending as many leaders out the door as quickly as they are equipped. Instead of stockpiling volunteer talent, these churches accept that there will be frequent "valley times" in the quantity and quality of leaders, particularly after sending out a significant-sized church plant.

Tension #11: Relational Stability vs. Relational Transience
Should we focus on developing the current social networks of friendship within the mother church or potentially disrupt those relationships through sending?

Planting a church can, and will, seriously disrupt existing social networks of friendship, especially when staff and volunteer leaders who demonstrate love and care for your church are sent out. Circles of friends can lose their cohesiveness as some friends go to seed the church plant, while others stay with the mother church. The temptation is to stop or slow planting so that the body can become more socially connected and attached to one another. If you're going to be a leader of a multiplying church, you must help your church understand the true basis for unity.

Tension #12: Systems Optimized vs. Systems Dispersed
Should we direct energy toward optimizing systems at the mother church, or toward the system and people at a new church plant?

Ministry excellence is a worthy goal. God deserves our very best, and as leaders we have to develop God-honoring systems through each ministry of our church. Multiplication culture-builders, though, are careful not to allow this pursuit of optimization to prevent them from releasing leaders and resources. When staff, leaders and workers are released for planting endeavors, systems are usually impacted in their operational efficiency. But take heart! This disruption allows your church to be disbursed to new places of growth.

Tension #13: Board Wisdom vs. Board Faith
Should our board lean more on cautious wisdom or risk-taking faith?

This tension depends on the polity and governance under which your church operates. Certainly, wisdom and faith are not opposites. They can, and should, coexist in the mind of a truly spiritual person. Though this tension is usually tied in some way to financial considerations, it is about much more than finances.

Church boards rightly concern themselves with church sustainability. When ministry actions that seemingly threaten sustainability are proposed, most boards have a natural protectiveness to resist. They cite the priority of wisdom: "God has given us brains to understand the realities we have to live with." Rare is the board that can reach forward in faith and risk what exists for the sake of Kingdom multiplication. These unique board leaders say, "This makes little sense in the natural, but we prayerfully believe God is going to back us up. Consequently, we will take action for Kingdom multiplication."

Tension #14: Proximity Protection vs. Proximity Evangelism
Should the mother church protect our "turf" by sending the plant far away, or trust that working together will create greater Kingdom impact?

You've probably heard the reasons for planting a certain distance (e.g., 30 minutes, 20 miles) away from the mother church:

• We don't want to saturate the market;
• You'll be competing with us;
• We need our best leaders to stay with us;
• You don't want to be a "sheep stealer, do you?" etc.

Addition-growth culture might view the "fishing pool" as members of the mother church or existing Christian consumers looking for a new church in the local area. Leaders who respond from a multiplication worldview, though, believe the fishing pool consists of hungry unbelievers and the unchurched in the area. Rather than struggling with transfer growth, rapidly multiplying churches are planted for evangelism to the unreached—in which case, even more churches could be planted in that area.

Tension #15: Highly Educated Planters vs. Spiritually Empowered Planters

Should our planters rely on accumulated knowledge or activated faith?

Because church planting is such a demanding undertaking, you'll naturally want to equip planters as much as possible. Inevitably, multiplying churches will face this tension: "Who is ready to plant? We should not send out a planter until they are fully equipped, seminary trained, theologically and intellectually astute, fully prepared for the work." However, be careful not to reinforce a false dichotomy between lay leaders and the "paid professionals." Don't hobble multiplication at the gate by creating non-scriptural qualifications for who can and cannot plant.

The other extreme bases qualifications on those who are saved, gifted, able to gather people, enthusiastic and evangelistic—and therefore, ready to be sent. In the urgency of sending planters, though, be sure not to hinder planting by sending out zealous yet unqualified leaders who undermine healthy multiplication in the long term.

Tension #16: Filling Existing Churches vs. Starting New Churches

Should we prioritize revitalizing existing churches, or begin planting new churches?

For most planters, the reality is that there will already be local churches in the area where they feel called to plant. And many of those existing churches will be in need of revitalization. Multiplying leaders are open to collaborating with and blessing other local churches, but are not constrained by the needs of those existing churches. We should aggressively look for the opportunities to collaborate in planting and revitalization, rather than pitting the two against each other.

Tension #17: Missional Focus vs. Multiplication Focus
Should we address the needs of our neighborhood before starting a church, or address the community's needs at the same time as planting?

Walkemeyer writes about this tension and shares what he has learned through Light & Life Fellowship's multiplication journey: "The missional nature of the Church is undeniable. We are saved to serve, to demonstrate the tangible Kingdom, to be salt and light where God has placed us," he writes. "However, when that becomes an argument against the multiplication of churches, we have overthrown our point. Do we care for the poor *or* evangelize the lost? The answer is *yes*. As soon as the missional and multiplication become competitive, we have misunderstood the nature of both."

Multiplying leaders recognize God's heart for the poor and see that a missional emphasis can be the impetus for starting new churches. Out of missional expressions of the existing church, new churches can rise up and multiply missional endeavors.

Tension #18: Missions Focus vs. Multiplication Focus
Should we direct resources to global missions or to local church planting?

In response to the call to radical multiplication, you'll likely experience others' hesitation. It might go something like this: "Why should we start new churches to tell people about Jesus when there are numerous ways for Americans to hear the gospel? Most have heard it multiple times. Instead, we need to focus on taking the gospel to those who have never heard it for the first time!"

Multiplying leaders refuse to believe that resources dedicated to local church planting will detract from global missions. These leaders believe every new church has the potential to become a resource for global missions.

Epilogue

I can't help but feel a sense of anticipation as Exponential looks ahead to this next year and focuses on what it will take to move the needle of multiplication.

What will today's churches and our cities look like if micro-addition and macro-multiplication become second nature in an increasing number of churches? How will our mission to make disciples be impacted if a significant number of churches commit to multiplication as a core value, face the tensions head-on and begin to develop a thriving culture of multiplication growth? Pause just a moment and think about what our world—and your children's and grandchildren's world—would look like if churches have to intentionally try *not* to multiply and the Lord added to our numbers daily.

We have an opportunity to buck status quo and embrace the values of the early Church (Acts 2:42-47). In your lifetime, you have the opportunity to ignite a culture of multiplication and lead a church planting movement that both makes disciples (the micro) *and* multiplies churches (the macro). Let that sink in … .

As you know by now after reading this book, a multiplication culture requires a core conviction on your part to multiply and an understanding of what it takes to create and nurture a specific culture through the alignment of your values, narrative and practices. When the tensions come (and they *will* come, as many of the leaders featured in this book series will affirm), your core convictions to multiply—and the culture you've created—will determine if you'll settle for the status quo or lead a multiplying church that as multiplying leader Larry Walkemeyer says in chapter four, "builds a different scoreboard—one that lights up when new leaders are sent out instead of simply when new consumers come in. The glory of the local church gets lost in the glory of the Kingdom."

As you think toward the future of what it means to you and your church to embrace multiplication and build a new scoreboard, our sincere prayer is that you grasp what it looks like to become a multiplying church, as well as be the leader of one. To that end, we have purposed to show church planters that a DNA of multiplication *is* possible. More than that, it's what God designed for His Church.

Related Resources

Throughout 2015 and beyond, we'll be sharing stories and examples of multiplying churches through this eBook series and through our 2015 Exponential Conference theme, "Spark: Igniting a Culture of Multiplication."

eBooks

20+ new FREE eBooks are being added via this new library. Authors include Larry Walkemeyer, JD Greear, Ralph Moore, KP Yohannan, AJ Lall, Darrin Patrick, Steve Stroope, and many more. These leaders of multiplying churches share their journey of creating a culture of multiplication growth.

These eBooks are in addition to 60+ existing FREE eBooks in our library. Check http://my.exponential.org/ebooks for new releases.

Exponential Conferences

The theme of our 2015 Exponential East (Tampa) and West (Southern CA) conferences is SPARK: Igniting a Culture of Multiplication. Join thousands of other leaders as we pursue a better understanding of how to use our tensions to cultivate a culture of multiplication. Visit exponential.org/2015east or exponential.org/2015west to learn more.

Social Media

Twitter - @churchplanting

Facebook - Facebook.com/churchplanting

RSS - http://feeds.feedburner.com/exponential

Author Biography

Todd Wilson currently serves as the Director of Exponential (exponential.org). Todd is passionate about the local church and the starting of healthy, high-impact new churches. He enjoys starting new things that are focused on Kingdom impact and multiplication. He also enjoys helping others create an image of future possibilities and the strategy to implement them.

Todd received his BS in nuclear engineering from North Carolina State University and a master's degree equivalent from the Bettis Atomic Power Laboratory. He spent 15 years serving in the Division of Naval Reactors on nuclear submarine design, operation, maintenance, and overhaul.

After a two-year wrestling match with God, Todd entered full-time vocational ministry as the Executive Pastor at New Life Christian Church. Todd played a visionary and strategic role for several years as New Life grew and implemented key initiatives such as multi-site, externally focused, and church planting. Increasingly Todd became passionate about starting healthy new churches and now spends most of his energy engaged in a wide range of leading edge and pioneering initiatives aimed at helping catalyze movements of healthy, reproducing churches.

Todd is a founding member and Director of Exponential. Exponential's core focus is distributing thought leadership in the form of conferences, books, podcasts, software, and small group learning communities.

Todd is a certified Life Planner and strategically invests in the lives of several leaders and organizations each year.

Todd lives in Manassas, VA with his wife Anna (happily married for over 25 years) and their two boys, Ben and Chris.

**EXPONENTIAL
CONFERENCE
2015**

April 27-30 | Tampa, FL
October 5-8 | Los Angeles. CA

At **Exponential 2015** we will pursue together how to use our **Tensions** to shape a **Culture** of **Multiplication**

- 100+ Speakers
- 9 Tracks
- 5000 Church Planting Leaders
- 10+ Pre-Conference Forums & Labs
- 20+ Bonus Sessions

REGISTER AT:
exponential.org/2015